SCHOLASTIC

Instant Practice Packets
Numbers & Counting

Joan Novelli & Holly Grundon

New York • Toronto • London • Auckland • Sydney
Mexico City • New Delhi • Hong Kong • Buenos Aires

Teaching *Resources*

Photograph, page 4, copyright © 2011 by Rosemary Novelli Tomas. Used by permission.

"Grab-Bag Math" on page 6 originally appeared in *Irresistible 1, 2, 3s: 50 Easy, Fun, Multisensory Activities to Help All Kids Explore and Learn Numbers* by Joan Novelli (Scholastic, 2000). Used by permission of the author.

Edited by Immacula A. Rhodes

Cover design by Wendy Chan

Interior design by Joan Novelli and Holly Grundon

Interior illustrations by Teresa Anderko, Maxie Chambliss, Rusty Fletcher, and Brian LaRossa

ISBN: 978-0-545-30587-7

Interior design and text copyright © 2011 by Joan Novelli and Holly Grundon.

Illustrations copyright © 2011 by Scholastic Inc.

Published by Scholastic Inc.

All rights reserved.

Printed in the U.S.A.

2 3 4 5 6 7 8 9 10   40   18 17 16 15 14 13 12 11

Contents

Number & Counting Packets

Introduction

IT'S my birthday!" says Ricardo, holding up five fingers to show how old he is now. Birthdays are often among a child's first experiences with numbers. Young children cheerfully display fingers on their hands when someone asks how old they are, count candles on cakes, and routinely want to know "How many more days?" until their next birthday. Their lives are filled with authentic experiences such as these that naturally involve mathematical thinking on a daily basis. Children notice numbers everywhere and make connections ("Hey! There's a 5 on that sign, and I'm five!"). They count all sorts of things (eyes and ears, buttons on a shirt, peas on a plate), know who has the same, more, or less ("Katrina has more crackers than me!"), and understand representation (setting the table with a napkin and cup for each person). All the while, they're constructing mathematical understandings that will allow them to successfully handle the more sophisticated skills and concepts to come.

Number and Operations is "at the core" of a preK–2 math program (NCTM, 2000). Research shows that "specific quantitative and numerical knowledge in the years before first grade has been found to be a stronger predictor of later mathematics achievement than tests of intelligence or memory abilities" (Krajewski, 2005, as cited in Sarama & Clements, 2009). With reproducible activity packets that target the numbers 1 though 30, *Instant Practice Packets: Numbers & Counting* offers instructional support for helping children build a solid foundation for success with math. In addition to providing practice with number formation, the activities are designed to promote overall number sense—from counting and recognizing how many are in a set to sequencing and exploring relationships between numbers. Additional features in each packet include:

- multisensory activities that reflect research about the way children learn—for example, the hand-sign component of each packet adds a kinesthetic connection

- pictures to support connections between numbers and the quantities they represent

- opportunities to revisit skills and concepts, deepen understanding, and develop flexible thinking

- kid-friendly layouts that keep interest high

TEACHING TIP

Page 1 of each packet features number-formation practice. For children who are left-handed, consider writing the target number at the end (right side) of each practice line to provide a model they can easily see as they practice tracing and writing the number.

Instant Practice Packets: Numbers & Counting • © 2011 by Joan Novelli & Holly Grundon • Scholastic Teaching Resources

Teaching With the Numbers & Counting Packets

The packets in this book are organized in order from 1 to 30, but can be used in any sequence to meet your instructional needs. To prepare the packets for use, photocopy the pages and staple to bind. Introduce the packets by "walking through" each page with children. Review each activity and model how to complete it. The packets allow children to work at their own pace, and taking time in advance to review directions will facilitate their independence. Following is an overview of each page.

PAGE 1: The first page of each packet introduces the target number and provides guided practice for tracing and writing the number. Point out the guide arrows to students and model using them to form each number correctly. Through a variety of fonts, children also see that there are different styles for writing the same number, and they take a turn creating a number style all their own! (Encourage creativity as children "design" a new way to write the number.) Children also learn how to use hand signs as another way to form numbers. This kinesthetic component further reinforces and expands children's understanding of numbers.

PAGE 2: "Fun With Numbers" features five mini-activities that reinforce number sense. Children practice writing the target number, then circle it in a "number hunt." As children complete this activity, remind them to look for the target number three times. They work with number sequences by counting up and back, and they count hippos, horses, and other creatures to identify the number that tells "how many."

PAGE 3: "Count Your Pennies" lets children apply their knowledge about numbers to real-life situations—in this case, counting pennies to make a "purchase." "Count and Compare" reinforces number sense, including an understanding of the relative magnitude of numbers.

PAGE 4: "What Do You Know?" offers a self-assessment as children use pictures and words to share what they know about the target number. "Bubble Time" provides practice with multiple-choice style questions, while helping children review the target number and, in most cases, numbers leading up to that number.

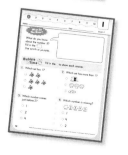

Activities to Extend Learning

Children will enjoy taking their number and counting experiences further with the following activities.

Book Shares

Consider the following suggestions, adapted from *The New Kindergarten: Teaching Reading, Writing, and More* (Leuenberger, 2003), for using children's literature to support mathematical thinking.

Act It Out: After sharing children's books that make connections to math concepts, engage children in dramatizing story events. Adding this kinesthetic component offers another way to understand math concepts, while also reinforcing comprehension skills. Books such as *The Doorbell Rang* by Pat Hutchins (Greenwillow, 1986) and *Five Little Monkeys Jumping on the Bed* by Eileen Christelow (Clarion, 1989) are perfect choices for reinforcing number sense through dramatizations.

Innovations on a Story: Share Tasha Tudor's *1 Is One* (Simon & Schuster, 1956), the Caldecott-Honor classic that counts from 1 to 20 with rhyming text and charming illustrations ("*1* is one duckling swimming in a dish; *2* is two sisters making a wish…"). Then use the story as a model for creating new rhymes for numbers—for example, "*1* is one cat, curled up on a chair; *2* is two sneakers; that makes a pair!" Have children illustrate the rhymes to make a class book.

Counting by Threes: Fairy tales often have elements or events that come in threes. Share favorite retellings, such as *Goldilocks and the Three Bears* by Jan Brett (Putnam, 1996) and *The True Story of the Three Little Pigs* by John Scieszka (Viking, 1989). Stock a math center with child-drawn pictures of important characters and events from the stories. Guide children to use the pictures in activities that reinforce math skills, such as one-to-one matching (chairs and bears) and counting by threes (chairs, bears, pigs, and so on).

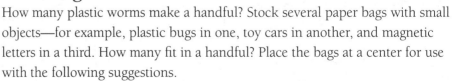

Grab-Bag Math

How many plastic worms make a handful? Stock several paper bags with small objects—for example, plastic bugs in one, toy cars in another, and magnetic letters in a third. How many fit in a handful? Place the bags at a center for use with the following suggestions.

- Have two children each take a handful from one bag. Ask: *Who has more?* Let children share guesses, then match their objects one-to-one to find out. Repeat with handfuls from different bags.

Discuss reasons that a handful of one object might amount to more or less than a handful of another.

- Have children take a handful in both hands from one bag. How do they think the handfuls compare? Have them line up the items one-to-one to find out.

- Set up a chart for children to record how many of each object they fit in a handful. Ask questions to promote mathematical thinking—for example, "How many children fit 10 toy cars in a handful? How about 10 plastic spiders?"

Taking Inventory

This activity, adapted from *Integrating Math Into the Early Childhood Curriculum* (Milstein & Martin, 2007), encourages the use of math language as children "take inventory" of materials in the classroom and practice counting, comparing, and more in the process.

1. To make a reusable sorting mat, use brightly colored tape to divide a plain plastic tablecloth into sections, as shown above. Label index cards with numbers from 1 to 20 (several cards per number), adjusting the range as needed.

2. Choose items to sort, such as plastic foods and utensils from the dramatic play center. Place one of each item in a section on the sorting mat to create "labels" (or use words, as shown above).

3. Have children take turns placing items on the sorting mat. Along the way, help them make comparisons—for example, ask: "Are there more spoons or markers so far?"

4. When the sorting is complete, have children place a number card in each section to show how many items are in that section.

5. Place the sorting mat and number cards at a center, and provide bins with pre-selected collections for children to sort, such as blocks (by shape), books (by theme or author), and crayons (by color).

TEACHING TIP

The word *number* is often used interchangeably with *numeral*, and for young children, differentiating between the two may create confusion. As children grow in their understanding of number concepts, they can learn that a numeral is a symbol that represents a number or idea— for example, when writing the date as month/day/year, as with 9/25/2012, the numeral *9* represents September, the ninth month of the year. To further develop math vocabulary, children can learn that a digit is a single numeral—the numeral *9* has one digit (9), while *25* has two digits (2 and 5).

Count and Compare

Set up a hands-on version of the "Count and Compare" activity (page 3 in each packet) to encourage use of math language and understanding of numerical relations.

1. Group children in pairs. Give each pair a set of "greater than," "less than," and "equal to" cards (write each symbol on an index card) and two bags of counters (use the same number but different color or type in each bag—for example, 10 red counters in one bag and 10 blue counters in the other).

2. Have one partner set up a "Count and Compare" problem by using some (or all) of the counters from one bag to create one set, and some (or all) from the other bag to create a second set.

3. Have the other child count the objects in each set and place the correct symbol card between the sets to show how they compare. Then partners switch roles and repeat. As a variation, children can do the same thing with small objects such as crayons or playing cards.

• •

Connections to the Standards

The activities in *Instant Practice Packets: Numbers & Counting* are aligned with the Number and Operations standard for grades preK–2 as outlined by the National Council of Teachers of Mathematics (NCTM) in its *Principles and Standards for School Mathematics* (2000), and support the following expectations:

• count with understanding and recognize "how many" in sets

• develop understanding of the relative position and magnitude of whole numbers

• develop a sense of whole numbers and represent and use them in flexible ways

• connect number words and numerals to the quantities they represent

The activities also correlate with the math standards recommended by the Common Core State Standards Initiative, a state-led effort to establish a single set of clear educational standards aimed at providing students with a high-quality education. At the time this book went to press, these standards were in the process of being finalized. To learn more, go to www.corestandards.org.

References & Resources

Leuenberger, C. (2003). *The new kindergarten: Teaching reading, writing, and more*. New York: Scholastic.

Milstein, V., & Martin, J. (2007). *Integrating math into the early childhood curriculum*. New York: Scholastic.

National Council of Teachers of Mathematics. (2000). *Principles and standards for school mathematics*. Reston, VA: National Council of Teachers of Mathematics.

Northwest Regional Educational Laboratory (2005). "Focus on effectiveness." Retrieved January 10, 2011 from <http://www.netc.org>.

Novelli, J. (2000). *Irresistible 1, 2, 3s: 50 easy, fun, multisensory activities to help all kids explore and learn numbers*. New York: Scholastic.

Sarama, J., & Clements, D. H. (2009). *Early childhood mathematics education research: Learning trajectories for young children*. Routledge: New York.

Name: _____   Date: _____

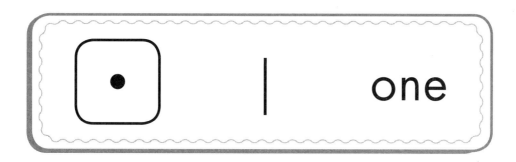

one

Write the number 1.

The number **1** can look like this.

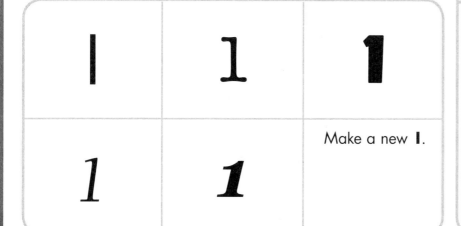

Make a new **1**.

Sign It!

You can use hand shapes to make numbers. Try making a **1**!

Name: _____ Date: _____

Fun With Numbers

Write the number.

:

one

Circle each 1.

1   3   5   4
  6   2   1
8   1   7   9

Count up!

___ 2 3 4 5

Circle the number that tells how many.

2   1   3

Count back!

5 4 3 2 ___

Name: _____ Date: _____ page 3

Count Your Pennies

Color the pennies you need to buy the bear.
Write the number.

_____ ¢

Count and Compare

How many balloons are in each set?
Write the number. Fill in **>**, **<**, or **=**.

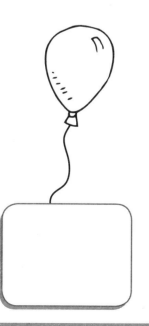 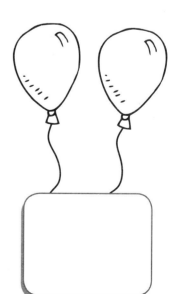

_____

Name: _____ Date: _____

What Do You Know?

What do you know
about the number **1**?
Fill in the ⬜.
Use words or pictures.

Bubble Time

Fill in the ○ to show each answer.

1. Which set has 1?

   ○

   ○

   ○

2. Which set has more than 1?

   ○

   ○

   ○

3. Which number comes
   just before 2?

   ○ 1

   ○ 2

   ○ 4

4. Which number is missing?

   ○ 1

   ○ 4

   ○ 2

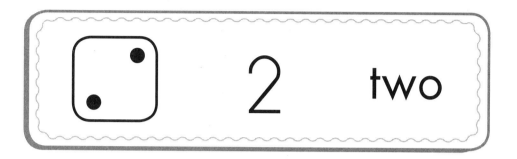

2   two

Write the number **2**.

The number **2** can look like this.

2	2	**2**
2	**2**	Make a new **2**.

Sign It!

You can use hand shapes to make numbers. Try making a **2**!

Name: _____   Date: _____

Fun With Numbers

Write the number.

two

Circle each 2.

5   4   6   2

2   3   1

7   9   2   8

Count up!

1 ___ 3 4 5

Circle the number
that tells how many.

2   1   3

Count back!

5 4 3 ___ 1

Name: _____   Date: _____   **page 3**

Count Your Pennies

Color the pennies you need to buy the pencil.
Write the number.

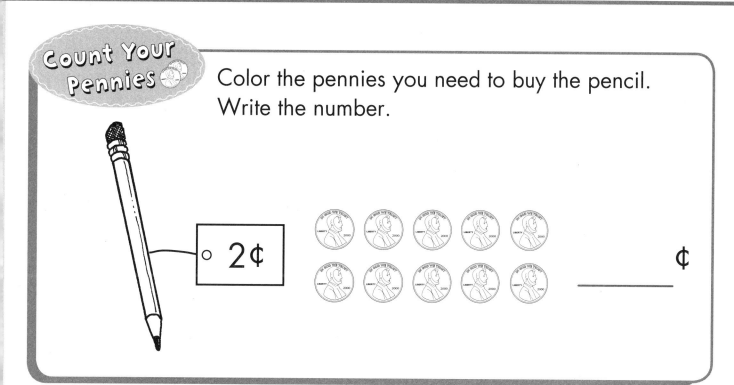

○ **2¢**

_____ ¢

Count and Compare

How many balloons are in each set?
Write the number. Fill in **>**, **<**, or **=**.

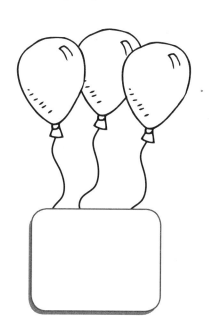

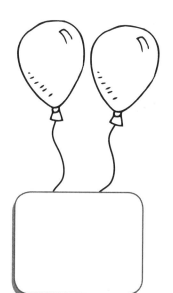

_____

Name: _____   Date: _____   page 4

What Do You Know?

What do you know about the number **2**? Fill in the ☐.
Use words or pictures.

Bubble Time Fill in the ○ to show each answer.

1. Which set has 2?

   ○

   ○

   ○

2. Which set has more than 2?

   ○

   ○

   ○

3. Which number comes just after 1?

   ○ 1

   ○ 2

   ○ 4

4. Which numbers are missing?

   ○ 4 and 5

   ○ 1 and 2

   ○ 3 and 4

Instant Practice Packets: Numbers & Counting • © 2011 by Joan Novelli & Holly Grundon • Scholastic Teaching Resources

Name: _____ Date: _____

3   three

Write the number **3**.

The number **3** can look like this.

3	3	**3**
3	*3*	Make a new **3**.

Sign It!

You can use hand shapes to make numbers. Try making a **3**!

Fun With Numbers

Write the number.

three

Circle each 3.

7   3   6   5
  4   3   1
3   2   8   9

Count up!

1   2   ___   4   5

Count back!

5   4   ___   2   1

Circle the number
that tells how many.

1   2   3

Instant Practice Packets: Numbers & Counting • © 2011 by Joan Novelli & Holly Grundon • Scholastic Teaching Resources

Name: _____ Date: _____

Count Your Pennies

Color the pennies you need to buy the baseball.
Write the number.

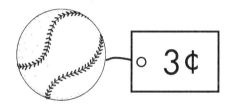

_____ ¢

Count and Compare

How many balloons are in each set?
Write the number. Fill in **>**, **<**, or **=**.

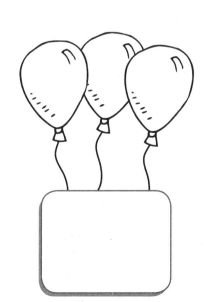

_____

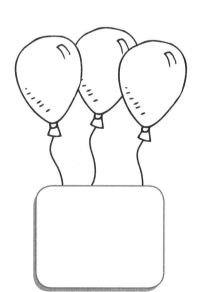

Name: _____ Date: _____

What Do You Know?

What do you know about the number **3**?
Fill in the ⬜.
Use words or pictures.

Bubble Time

Fill in the ○ to show each answer.

1. Which set has 3?

   ○

   ○

   ○

2. Which set has more than 2?

   ○

   ○

   ○

3. Which number comes just before 3?

   ○ 1

   ○ 3

   ○ 2

4. Which numbers are missing?

   ○ 1 and 4

   ○ 2 and 3

   ○ 4 and 5

Instant Practice Packets: Numbers & Counting • © 2011 by Joan Novelli & Holly Grundon • Scholastic Teaching Resources

Name: _____ Date: _____

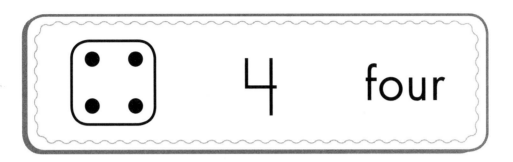

4 four

Write the number 4.

The number **4** can look like this.

4	4	**4**
4	*4*	Make a new **4**.

Sign It!

You can use hand shapes to make numbers. Try making a **4**!

Fun With Numbers

Write the number.

4

four

Circle each 4.

1   4   3   5

7   2   4

4   8   9   6

Count up!

1   2   3 ___ 5

Circle the number
that tells how many.

2   4   1

Count back!

5 ___   3   2   1

Name: _____ Date: _____ page 3

Count Your Pennies

Color the pennies you need to buy the bell.
Write the number.

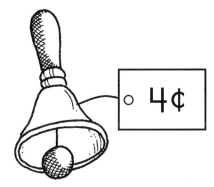

4¢

_____ ¢

Count and Compare

How many balloons are in each set?
Write the number. Fill in **>**, **<**, or **=**.

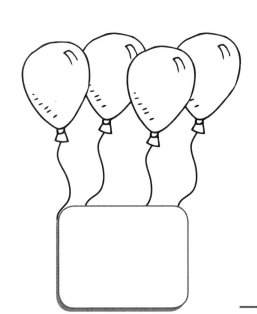

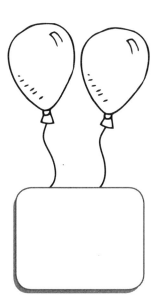

_____

Instant Practice Packets: Numbers & Counting • © 2011 by Joan Novelli & Holly Grundon • Scholastic Teaching Resources

Name: _____   Date: _____

What Do You Know?

What do you know about the number **4**?
Fill in the ▢.
Use words or pictures.

Bubble Time

Fill in the ○ to show each answer.

1. Which set has 4?

○

○

○

2. Which set has more than 3?

○

○

○

3. Which number comes just before 4?

○ 2

○ 3

○ 1

4. Which numbers are missing?

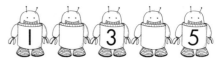

○ 1 and 3

○ 3 and 5

○ 2 and 4

Name: _____ Date: _____

Write the number **5**.

The number **5** can look like this.

5	5	**5**
5	*5*	Make a new **5**.

Sign It!

You can use hand shapes to make numbers. Try making a **5**!

Name: _____ Date: _____ page 2

Fun With Numbers

Write the number.

five

Circle each 5.

1   2   5   3

5   4   6

7   8   9   5

Count up!

1   2   3   4   ___

Circle the number
that tells how many.

| 1 | 3 | 5 |

Count back!

___   4   3   2   1

Name: _____ Date: _____

Count Your Pennies

Color the pennies you need to buy the yo-yo.
Write the number.

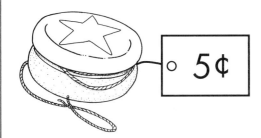

_____ ¢

Count and Compare

How many balloons are in each set?
Write the number. Fill in **>**, **<**, or **=**.

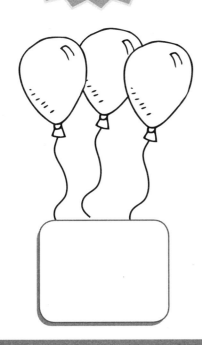

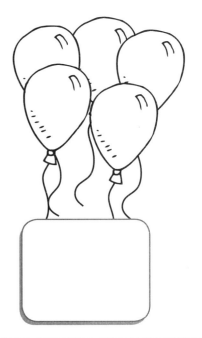

_____

Name: _____ Date: _____ page 4

What Do You Know?

What do you know about the number **5**?
Fill in the ⬜.
Use words or pictures.

Bubble Time Fill in the ○ to show each answer.

---

1. Which set has 5?

   ○

   ○

   ○

2. Which set has more than 3?

   ○

   ○

   ○

---

3. Which number comes just before 5?

   ○ 1

   ○ 3

   ○ 4

4. Which numbers are missing?

   ○ 1 and 4

   ○ 2 and 5

   ○ 3 and 5

Instant Practice Packets: Numbers & Counting • © 2011 by Joan Novelli & Holly Grundon • Scholastic Teaching Resources

Name: _____ Date: _____

Write the number **6**.

The number **6** can look like this.

Make a new **6**.

Instant Practice Packets: Numbers & Counting • © 2011 by Joan Novelli & Holly Grundon • Scholastic Teaching Resources

Sign It!

You can use hand shapes to make numbers. Try making a **6**!

29

Name: _____ Date: _____

Fun With Numbers

Write the number.

six

Circle each 6.

2 3 6 5
6 4 7
1 8 10 6

Count up!

2 3 4 5 ___

Circle the number
that tells how many.

4   6   2

Count back!

___ 5 4 3 2

Name: _____   Date: _____   page 3

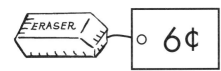 **Count Your Pennies**

Color the pennies you need to buy the eraser.
Write the number.

ERASER   ○ 6¢

_____ ¢

 **Count and Compare**

How many balloons are in each set?
Write the number. Fill in **>**, **<**, or **=**.

_____

Name: _____ Date: _____

What Do You Know?

What do you know about the number **6**?
Fill in the ☐.
Use words or pictures.

Bubble Time

Fill in the ○ to show each answer.

1. Which set has 6?

2. Which set has more than 4?

3. Which number comes just before 6?

○ 1

○ 3

○ 5

4. Which numbers are missing?

○ 1 and 2

○ 4 and 5

○ 3 and 6

Name: _____ Date: _____ page 1

7 seven

Write the number **7**.

The number **7** can look like this.

7	7	**7**
7	7	Make a new **7**.

Sign It!

You can use hand shapes to make numbers. Try making a **7**!

Fun With Numbers

Write the number.

7 [::: dots ::]

seven

Circle each 7.

8 9 3 7

7 2 4

6 1 7 5

Count up!

3 4 5 6 ___

Circle the number
that tells how many.

7   5   1

Count back!

___ 6 5 4 3

Name: _____   Date: _____

Count Your Pennies

Color the pennies you need to buy the cap.
Write the number.

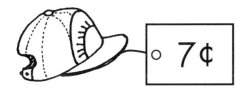

_____ ¢

Count and Compare

How many balloons are in each set?
Write the number. Fill in **>**, **<**, or **=**.

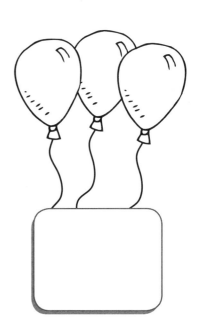

_____

What Do You Know?

What do you know
about the number **7**?
Fill in the ☐.
Use words or pictures.

Bubble Time   Fill in the ○ to show each answer.

1. Which set has 7?

○

○

○

2. Which set has more than 5?

○

○

○

3. Which number comes just before 7?

○ 4

○ 6

○ 2

4. Which numbers are missing?

○ 4 and 5

○ 1 and 2

○ 3 and 6

Instant Practice Packets: Numbers & Counting • © 2011 by Joan Novelli & Holly Grundon • Scholastic Teaching Resources

Name: _____ Date: _____

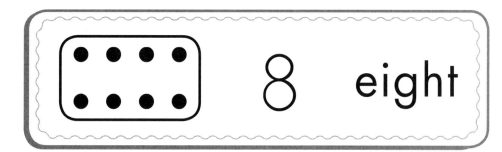

8 eight

Write the number **8**.

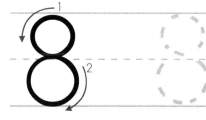

The number **8** can look like this.

8	8	**8**
8	*8*	Make a new **8**.

Sign It!

You can use hand shapes to make numbers. Try making an **8**!

Fun With Numbers

Write the number.

8

eight

Circle each 8.

8   1   3   5
  4   8   2
6   9   7   8

Count up!

4   5   6   7   ___

Circle the number
that tells how many.

6   7   8

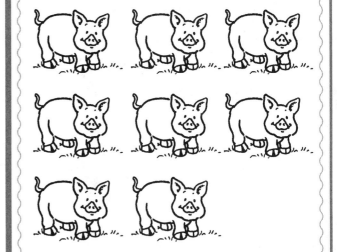

Count back!

___   7   6   5   4

Name: _____   Date: _____   page 3

Count Your Pennies

Color the pennies you need to buy the crayon.
Write the number.

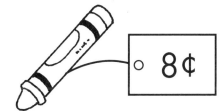   ○ **8¢**

_____ ¢

Count and Compare

How many balloons are in each set?
Write the number. Fill in **>**, **<**, or **=**.

_____

What Do You Know?

What do you know about the number **8**?
Fill in the ▢.
Use words or pictures.

Bubble Time

Fill in the ○ to show each answer.

1. Which set has 8?

○ 🐟🐟🐟🐟🐟🐟🐟🐟

○ 🐟🐟🐟🐟🐟

○ 🐟🐟🐟🐟

2. Which set has more than 6?

○ 🐢🐢🐢

○ 🐢🐢🐢🐢

○ 🐢🐢🐢🐢🐢🐢🐢🐢

3. Which number comes just before 8?

○ 1

○ 7

○ 3

4. Which numbers are missing?

○ 1 and 2

○ 6 and 8

○ 2 and 3

Name: _____ Date: _____ page 1

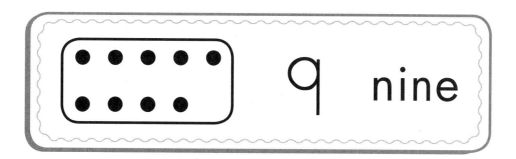

q nine

Write the number **9**.

The number **9** can look like this.

9	9	**9**
9	*9*	Make a new **9**.

Fun With Numbers

Write the number.

nine

Circle each 9.

6 2 5 9
4 9 7
1 8 9 3

Count up!

5 6 7 8 ___

Count back!

___ 8 7 6 5

Circle the number that tells how many.

9 3 8

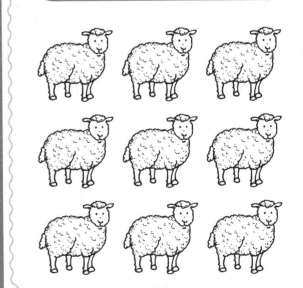

Name: _____ Date: _____

Count Your Pennies

Color the pennies you need to buy the drum.
Write the number.

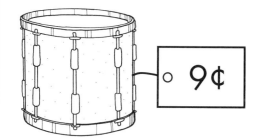

_____ ¢

Count and Compare

How many balloons are in each set?
Write the number. Fill in **>**, **<**, or **=**.

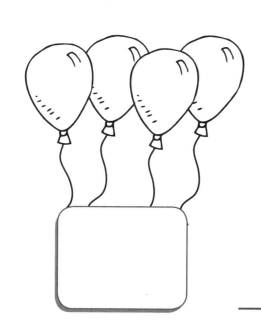

_____

Name: _____ Date: _____

What Do You Know?

What do you know
about the number **9**?
Fill in the .
Use words or pictures.

Bubble Time Fill in the ○ to show each answer.

1. Which set has 9?

○ 🐸🐸🐸

○ 🐸🐸🐸🐸🐸🐸

○ 🐸🐸🐸🐸🐸🐸🐸🐸🐸

2. Which set has more than 7?

○ 🚢🚢

○ 🚢🚢🚢🚢🚢🚢🚢🚢

○ 🚢🚢🚢🚢🚢

3. Which number comes just before 9?

○ 8

○ 3

○ 1

4. Which numbers are missing?

○ 5 and 6

○ 2 and 3

○ 1 and 4

Name: _____ Date: _____   page 1

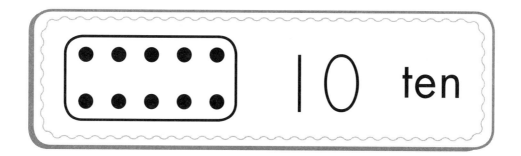

10 ten

Write the number 10.

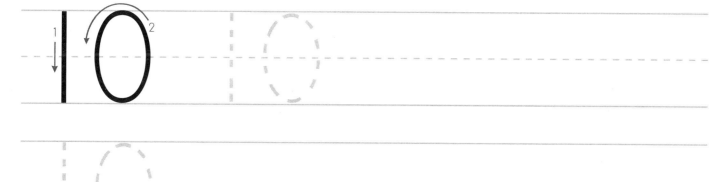

The number **10** can look like this.

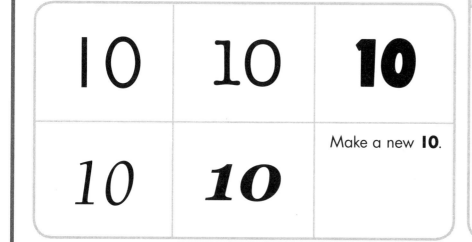

10	10

10

Make a new **10**.

Sign It!

Shake your thumb back and forth.

You can use hand shapes to make numbers. Try making a **10**!

Name: _____   Date: _____

Fun With Numbers

Write the number.

10   ten

Circle each 10.

7   10   8   3

5   9   10

10   4   6   2

Count up!

6 7 8 9 ___

Circle the number that tells how many.

5   10   1

Count back!

___ 9 8 7 6

Instant Practice Packets: Numbers & Counting • © 2011 by Joan Novelli & Holly Grundon • Scholastic Teaching Resources

Name: _____   Date: _____   page 3

Count Your Pennies

Color the pennies you need to buy the tape.
Write the number.

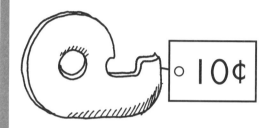

∘ 10¢

_____ ¢

Count and Compare

How many balloons are in each set?
Write the number. Fill in **>**, **<**, or **=**.

_____

Name: _____   Date: _____

What Do You Know?

What do you know about the number **10**?
Fill in the ☐.
Use words or pictures.

Bubble Time

Fill in the ○ to show each answer.

1. How many ▲?

   ▲ ▲ ▲ ▲ ▲ ▲ ▲ ▲ ▲ ▲

   ○ 7
   ○ 5
   ○ 10

2. Which numbers are missing?

   ○ 3 and 4
   ○ 9 and 10
   ○ 1 and 2

3. Which number comes just before 10?

   ○ 3
   ○ 7
   ○ 9

4. Which number is largest?

   ○ 8
   ○ 10
   ○ 1

Name: _____ Date: _____

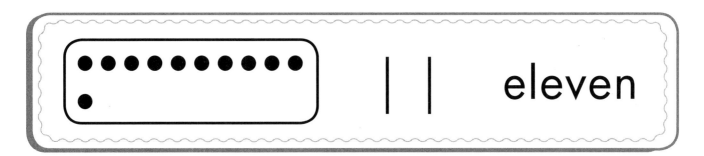

| | eleven

Write the number **| |**.

The number **| |** can look like this.

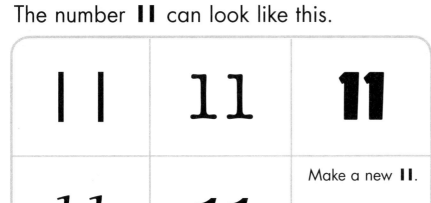

Make a new **| |**.

Sign It!

Snap your index finger up.

You can use hand shapes to make numbers. Try making an **| |**!

Name: _____ Date: _____ page 2

Fun With Numbers

Write the number.

: : :   ● ● ● ● ● ● ●
        ●

eleven

Circle each 11.

11 6 5 2
  7 9 11
4 8 11 10

Count up!

8 9 10 ___ 12

Count back!

12 ___ 10 9 8

Circle the number that tells how many.

9   5   11

Name: _____   Date: _____   page 3

Count Your Pennies

Color the pennies you need to buy the dinosaur.
Write the number.

_____ ¢

Count and Compare

How many balls are in each set?
Write the number. Fill in **>**, **<**, or **=**.

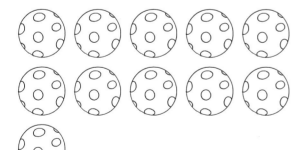

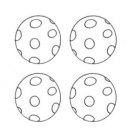

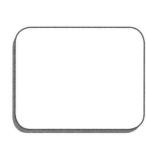

_____

Name: _____ Date: _____

What Do You Know?

What do you know about the number **11**?
Fill in the ⌐▢.
Use words or pictures.

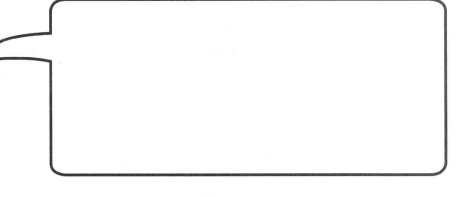

Bubble Time

Fill in the ○ to show each answer.

1. How many ▲?

▲ ▲ ▲ ▲ ▲ ▲ ▲ ▲ ▲ ▲
▲

○ 10
○ 7
○ 11

2. Which numbers are missing?

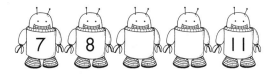

○ 3 and 4
○ 5 and 6
○ 9 and 10

3. Which number comes just before 11?

○ 7
○ 10
○ 3

4. Which number is largest?

○ 2
○ 9
○ 3

Instant Practice Packets: Numbers & Counting • © 2011 by Joan Novelli & Holly Grundon • Scholastic Teaching Resources

Name: _____   Date: _____

$|2$ twelve

Write the number 12.

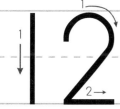

The number **12** can look like this.

12	12	**12**
12	***12***	Make a new **12**.

Sign It!

Snap your index finger and middle finger up.

You can use hand shapes to make numbers. Try making a **12**!

Fun With Numbers

Write the number.

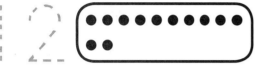

1 2

twelve

Circle each 12.

3   12   10   9

12   5   6

11   7   12   8

Count up!

8 9 10 11 ___

Circle the number
that tells how many.

12   7   8

Count back!

15 14 13 ___ 11

Instant Practice Packets: Numbers & Counting • © 2011 by Joan Novelli & Holly Grundon • Scholastic Teaching Resources

Count Your Pennies

Color the pennies you need to buy the truck.
Write the number.

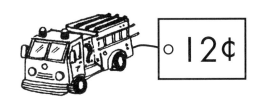

_____ ¢

Count and Compare

How many balls are in each set?
Write the number. Fill in **>**, **<**, or **=**.

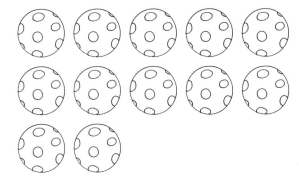

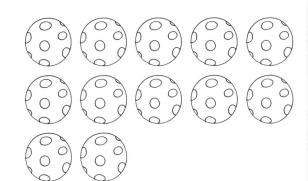

Name: _____ Date: _____

What Do You Know?

What do you know about the number **12**? Fill in the ⬚.
Use words or pictures.

Bubble Time

Fill in the ○ to show each answer.

1. How many ▲?

▲ ▲ ▲ ▲ ▲ ▲ ▲ ▲ ▲
▲ ▲

- ○ 12
- ○ 10
- ○ 8

2. Which numbers are missing?

8 ___ 10 11 ___

- ○ 2 and 5
- ○ 9 and 12
- ○ 3 and 7

3. Which number comes just before 12?

- ○ 11
- ○ 9
- ○ 3

4. Which number is largest?

- ○ 7
- ○ 5
- ○ 11

Instant Practice Packets: Numbers & Counting • © 2011 by Joan Novelli & Holly Grundon • Scholastic Teaching Resources

Name: _____ Date: _____

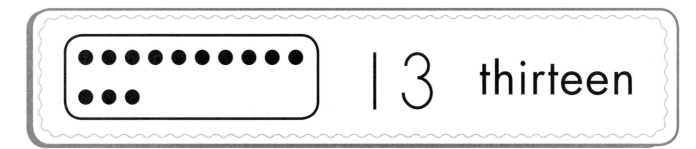

13 thirteen

Write the number 13.

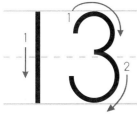

The number 13 can look like this.

Make a new 13.

Sign It!

Wiggle fingers twice.

You can use hand shapes to make numbers. Try making a **13**!

Name: _____   Date: _____

Fun With Numbers

Write the number.

13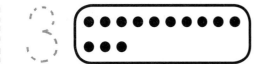

thirteen

Circle each 13.

14   12   13   9

11   10   7

13   5   1   13

Count up!

9 10 11 12 _____

Count back!

15 14 _____ 12 11

Circle the number
that tells how many.

3   10   13

   Instant Practice Packets: Numbers & Counting • © 2011 by Joan Novelli & Holly Grundon • Scholastic Teaching Resources

Name: _____   Date: _____

Count Your Pennies

Color the pennies you need to buy the car.
Write the number.

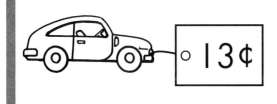

○ **13¢**

_____ ¢

Count and Compare

How many balls are in each set?
Write the number. Fill in **>**, **<**, or **=**.

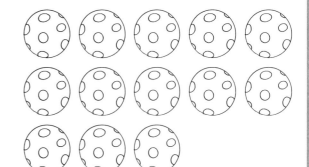

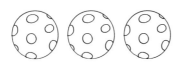

_____

Name: _____ Date: _____ page 4

What Do You Know?

What do you know about the number **13**?
Fill in the ☐.
Use words or pictures.

Bubble Time Fill in the ○ to show each answer.

1. How many ▲?

   ▲ ▲ ▲ ▲ ▲ ▲ ▲ ▲ ▲ ▲
   ▲ ▲ ▲

   ○ 12
   ○ 13
   ○ 7

2. Which numbers are missing?

   ○ 9 and 10
   ○ 5 and 6
   ○ 2 and 4

3. Which number comes just before 13?

   ○ 9
   ○ 10
   ○ 12

4. Which number is largest?

   ○ 11
   ○ 8
   ○ 2

Name: _____   Date: _____   page 1

14 fourteen

Write the number 14.

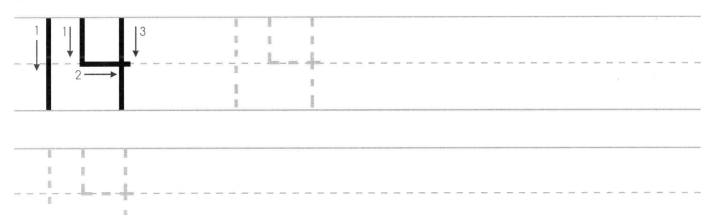

The number **14** can look like this.

14	14	**14**
14	*14*	Make a new **14**.

Sign It!

Wiggle fingers twice.

You can use hand shapes to make numbers. Try making a **14**!

Fun With Numbers

Write the number.

1 4

fourteen

Circle each 14.

14　11　5　10

13　4　6

14　7　14　12

Count up!

11　12　13 ___ 15

**Circle the number
that tells how many.**

12　14　6

Count back!

17　16　15 ___ 13

Instant Practice Packets: Numbers & Counting • © 2011 by Joan Novelli & Holly Grundon • Scholastic Teaching Resources

Name: _____   Date: _____   page 3

Count Your Pennies

Color the pennies you need to buy the crayons.
Write the number.

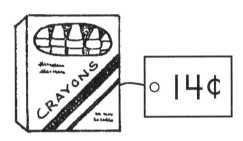

_____ ¢

Count and Compare

How many balls are in each set?
Write the number. Fill in **>**, **<**, or **=**.

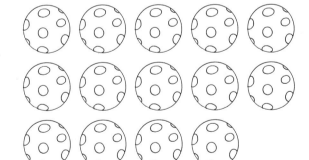

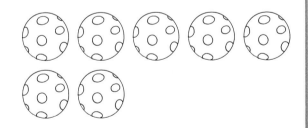

   _____

Name: _____ Date: _____ page 4

What Do You Know?

What do you know about the number **14**?
Fill in the ▭.
Use words or pictures.

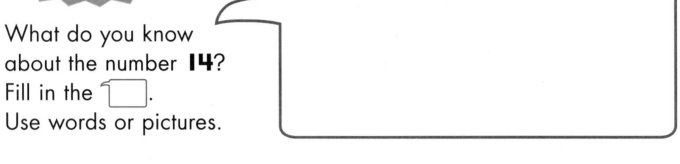

Bubble Time Fill in the ○ to show each answer.

1. How many ▲?

▲ ▲ ▲ ▲ ▲ ▲ ▲ ▲ ▲ ▲
▲ ▲ ▲ ▲

○ 10

○ 14

○ 9

2. Which numbers are missing?

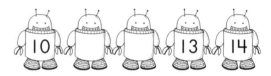

○ 8 and 9

○ 2 and 3

○ 11 and 12

3. Which number comes just before 14?

○ 11

○ 13

○ 10

4. Which number is largest?

○ 12

○ 6

○ 11

Instant Practice Packets: Numbers & Counting • © 2011 by Joan Novelli & Holly Grundon • Scholastic Teaching Resources

Name: _____   Date: _____

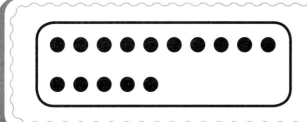

15 fifteen

Write the number **15**.

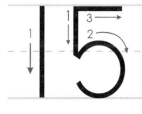

The number **15** can look like this.

15	15	**15**
15	***15***	Make a new **15**.

Sign It!

Wiggle fingers twice.

You can use hand shapes to make numbers. Try making a **15**!

Fun With Numbers

Write the number.

15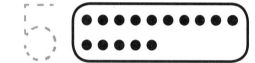

fifteen

Circle each 15.

6   15   11   13

5   9   15

10   15   14   2

Count up!

13   14   ____   16   17

Count back!

____   14   13   12   11

Circle the number that tells how many.

| 15 | 5 | 11 |

Name: _____   Date: _____   page 3

Count Your Pennies

Color the pennies you need to buy the flag.
Write the number.

○ 15¢

_____ ¢

Count and Compare

How many balls are in each set?
Write the number. Fill in **>**, **<**, or **=**.

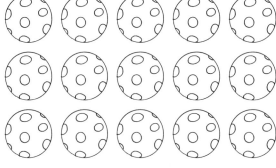

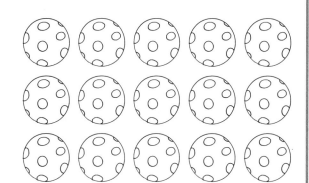

_____

Name: _____   Date: _____

What Do You Know?

What do you know about the number **15**?
Fill in the ⬜.
Use words or pictures.

Bubble Time   Fill in the ○ to show each answer.

1. How many ▲?

   ▲ ▲ ▲ ▲ ▲ ▲ ▲ ▲ ▲ ▲
   ▲ ▲ ▲ ▲ ▲

   ○ 10
   ○ 15
   ○ 5

2. Which numbers are missing?

   ○ 5 and 6
   ○ 8 and 9
   ○ 13 and 15

3. Which number comes just before 15?

   ○ 14
   ○ 10
   ○ 7

4. Which number is largest?

   ○ 7
   ○ 13
   ○ 10

Name: _____ Date: _____

16 sixteen

Write the number **16**.

The number **16** can look like this.

16	16	**16**
16	*16*	Make a new **16**.

Sign It!

You can use hand shapes to make numbers. Try making a **16**!

Name: _____   Date: _____   page 2

Fun With Numbers

Write the number.

16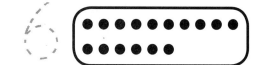

sixteen

Circle each 16.

16   9   10   7

8   14   16

12   6   16   15

Count up!

12   13   14   15   ____

Count back!

____   15   14   13   12

Circle the number that tells how many.

16   8   11

Instant Practice Packets: Numbers & Counting • © 2011 by Joan Novelli & Holly Grundon • Scholastic Teaching Resources

Name: _____ Date: _____ page 3

Count Your Pennies

Color the pennies you need to buy the flute.
Write the number.

16¢

_____ ¢

Count and Compare

How many balls are in each set?
Write the number. Fill in **>**, **<**, or **=**.

_____

Name: _____ Date: _____ page 4

What Do You Know?

What do you know about the number **16**? Fill in the ☐. Use words or pictures.

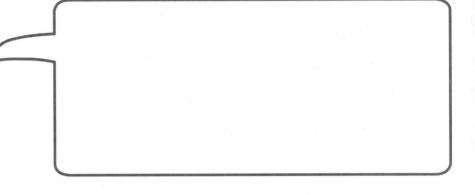

Bubble Time

Fill in the ○ to show each answer.

1. How many ▲?

   ▲ ▲ ▲ ▲ ▲ ▲ ▲ ▲ ▲
   ▲ ▲ ▲ ▲ ▲ ▲

   ○ 15
   ○ 2
   ○ 16

2. Which numbers are missing?

   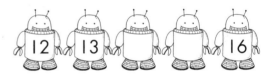

   ○ 14 and 15
   ○ 9 and 10
   ○ 7 and 8

3. Which number comes just before 16?

   ○ 11
   ○ 15
   ○ 3

4. Which number is largest?

   ○ 14
   ○ 4
   ○ 11

Name: _____ Date: _____

17 seventeen

Write the number **17**.

The number **17** can look like this.

17	17	**17**
17	*17*	Make a new **17**.

Sign It!

You can use hand shapes to make numbers. Try making a **17**!

Name: _____   Date: _____   page 2

Fun With Numbers

Write the number.

1 7   seventeen

Circle each 17.

17   10   11   9
8   17   16
15   13   12   17

Count up!

14   15   16   ___   18

Circle the number that tells how many.

5   13   17

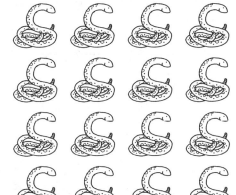

Count back!

20   19   18   ___   16

Name: _____ Date: _____ page 3

Count Your Pennies

Color the pennies you need to buy the rocket.
Write the number.

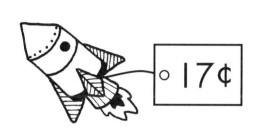

∘ 17¢

_____ ¢

Count and Compare

How many balls are in each set?
Write the number. Fill in **>**, **<**, or **=**.

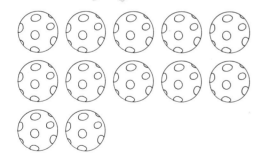

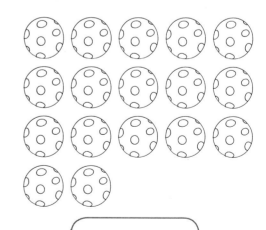

_____

Name: _____   Date: _____   page 4

What Do You Know?

What do you know about the number **17**? Fill in the ▢. Use words or pictures.

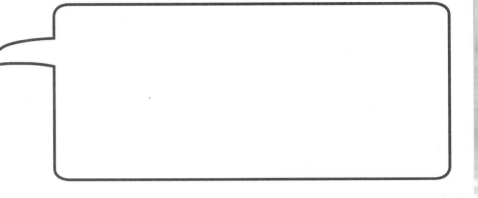

Bubble Time Fill in the ○ to show each answer.

1. How many ▲?

- ○ 17
- ○ 14
- ○ 8

2. Which numbers are missing?

- ○ 9 and 10
- ○ 16 and 17
- ○ 4 and 11

3. Which number comes just before 17?

- ○ 4
- ○ 12
- ○ 16

4. Which number is largest?

- ○ 15
- ○ 9
- ○ 14

Name: _____   Date: _____

 18 eighteen

Write the number 18.

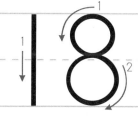

The number 18 can look like this.

18	18	**18**
18	***18***	Make a new 18.

Name: _____   Date: _____

Fun With Numbers

Write the number.

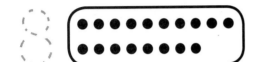

eighteen

Circle each 18.

18   17   15   6

10   9   18

3   14   18   12

Count up!

16   17   ___   19   20

Count back!

19   ___   17   16   15

Circle the number
that tells how many.

12   18   8

Instant Practice Packets: Numbers & Counting • © 2011 by Joan Novelli & Holly Grundon • Scholastic Teaching Resources

Name: _____ Date: _____ page 3

Count Your Pennies

Color the pennies you need to buy the book.
Write the number.

_____ ¢

Count and Compare

How many balls are in each set?
Write the number. Fill in **>**, **<**, or **=**.

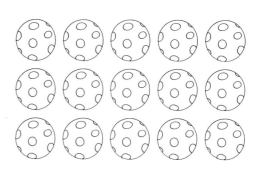

_____

Name: _____ Date: _____ page 4

What Do You Know?

What do you know about the number **18**?
Fill in the ☐.
Use words or pictures.

Bubble Time

Fill in the ○ to show each answer.

1. How many ▲?

○ 13
○ 18
○ 7

2. Which numbers are missing?

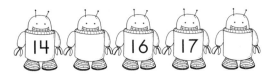

○ 15 and 18
○ 3 and 9
○ 10 and 12

3. Which number comes just before 18?

○ 11
○ 15
○ 17

4. Which number is largest?

○ 16
○ 6
○ 13

 nineteen

Write the number **19**.

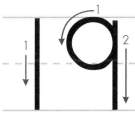

The number **19** can look like this.

19	19	**19**
19	***19***	Make a new **19**.

Sign It!

You can use hand shapes to make numbers. Try making a **19**!

Name: _____ Date: _____ page 2

Fun With Numbers

Write the number.

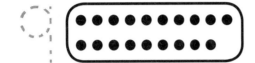

nineteen

Circle each 19.

15   18   19   17

19   14   19

13   12   11   10

Count up!

16 17 18 ___ 20

Circle the number
that tells how many.

9   11   19

Count back!

20 ___ 18 17 16

Name: _____ Date: _____ page 3

Count Your Pennies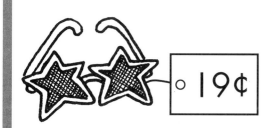

Color the pennies you need to buy the sunglasses.
Write the number.

_____ ¢

Count and Compare

How many balls are in each set?
Write the number. Fill in **>**, **<**, or **=**.

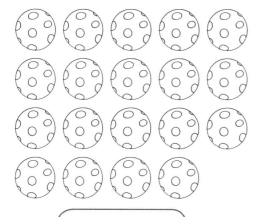

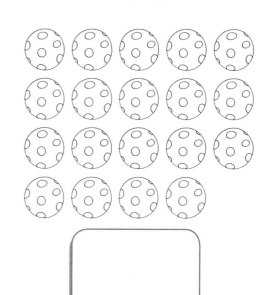

_____

Name: _____ Date: _____

What Do You Know?

What do you know about the number **19**?
Fill in the ☐.
Use words or pictures.

Bubble Time

Fill in the ○ to show each answer.

1. How many ▲?

   ○ 19
   ○ 2
   ○ 11

2. Which numbers are missing?

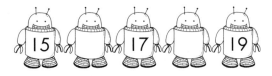

   ○ 2 and 8
   ○ 16 and 18
   ○ 12 and 13

3. Which number comes just before 19?

   ○ 18
   ○ 14
   ○ 16

4. Which number is largest?

   ○ 7
   ○ 5
   ○ 15

Name: _____   Date: _____

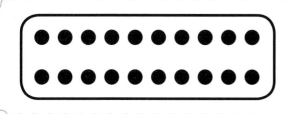

20   twenty

Write the number **20**.

The number **20** can look like this.

20	20	**20**
20	*20*	Make a new **20**.

Name: _____   Date: _____   page 2

Fun With Numbers

Write the number.

20 twenty

Circle each 20.

18   19   20   17
12   20   13
16   14   15   20

Count up!

16 17 18 19 ____

Circle the number
that tells how many.

20   10   5

Count back!

____ 19 18 17 16

Name: _____   Date: _____   page 3

Count Your Pennies

Color the pennies you need to buy the wand.
Write the number.

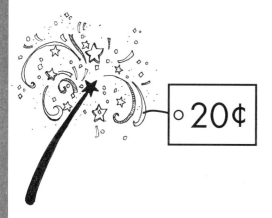

○ 20¢

_____ ¢

Count and Compare

How many balls are in each set?
Write the number. Fill in **>**, **<**, or **=**.

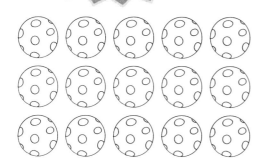

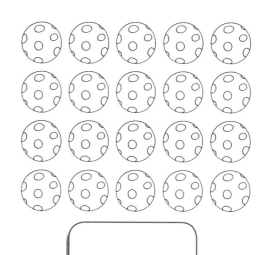

_____

Name: _____ Date: _____ page 4

What Do You Know?

What do you know about the number **20**?
Fill in the ⬜.
Use words or pictures.

Bubble Time Fill in the ○ to show each answer.

1. How many ▲?

- ○ 15
- ○ 10
- ○ 20

2. Which numbers are missing?

- ○ 13 and 14
- ○ 8 and 9
- ○ 18 and 20

3. Which number comes just before 20?

- ○ 19
- ○ 17
- ○ 11

4. Which number is largest?

- ○ 14
- ○ 18
- ○ 9

Instant Practice Packets: Numbers & Counting • © 2011 by Joan Novelli & Holly Grundon • Scholastic Teaching Resources

Name: _____ Date: _____

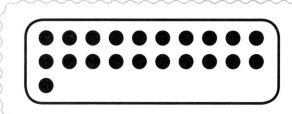

21   twenty-one

Write the number 21.

2 1

The number **21** can look like this.

2 1	21	**21**
21	*21*	Make a new **21**.

Sign It!

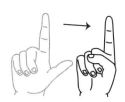

You can use hand shapes to make numbers. Try making a **21**!

Fun With Numbers

Write the number.

2̣1̣

twenty-one

Circle each 21.

2   10   18   21
   21   16   7
9   12   20   21

Count up!

18 19 20 ___ 22

Circle the number
that tells how many.

10   21   2

Count back!

22 ___ 20 19 18

Instant Practice Packets: Numbers & Counting • © 2011 by Joan Novelli & Holly Grundon • Scholastic Teaching Resources

Name: _____   Date: _____   page 3

Count Your Pennies

Color the pennies you need to buy the crown. Write the number.

○ 21¢

¢

_____

Count and Compare

How many crayons are in each set? Write the number. Fill in **>**, **<**, or **=**.

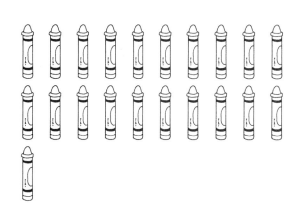

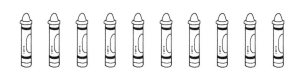

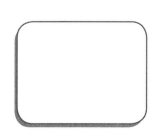

_____

Name: _____ Date: _____ page 4

What Do You Know?

What do you know about the number **21**?
Fill in the ☐.
Use words or pictures.

Bubble Time

Fill in the ○ to show each answer.

1. How many ▲?

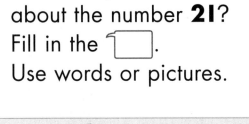

- ○ 20
- ○ 5
- ○ 21

2. Which numbers are missing?

- ○ 9 and 11
- ○ 13 and 16
- ○ 19 and 21

3. Which number comes just before 21?

- ○ 20
- ○ 9
- ○ 17

4. Which number is largest?

- ○ 14
- ○ 19
- ○ 4

Name: _____ Date: _____   page 1

22 twenty-two

Write the number **22**.

1↘ 1↘
2 2
2→ 2→

The number **22** can look like this.

22	22	**22**
22	**22**	Make a new **22**.

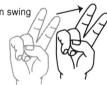

Fun With Numbers

Write the number.

22

twenty-two

Circle each 22.

3 16 22 19
11 15 1
22 20 8 22

Count up!

20 21 ___ 23 24

Circle the number
that tells how many.

22 12 6

Count back!

24 23 ___ 21 20

Name: _____ Date: _____ page 3

Count Your Pennies

Color the pennies you
need to buy the train.
Write the number.

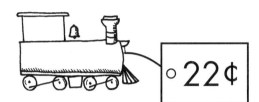

° 22¢

_____ ¢

Count and Compare

How many crayons are in each set?
Write the number. Fill in **>**, **<**, or **=**.

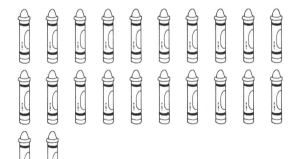

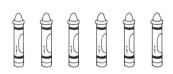

_____

Name: _____　Date: _____　page 4

What Do You Know?

What do you know about the number **22**?
Fill in the ☐.
Use words or pictures.

Bubble Time　Fill in the ○ to show each answer.

1. How many ▲?

▲ ▲ ▲ ▲ ▲ ▲ ▲ ▲ ▲ ▲
▲ ▲ ▲ ▲ ▲ ▲ ▲ ▲ ▲ ▲
▲ ▲

○ 22
○ 5
○ 12

2. Which numbers are missing?

○ 9 and 10
○ 19 and 20
○ 15 and 17

3. Which number comes just before 22?

○ 21
○ 8
○ 18

4. Which number is largest?

○ 19
○ 10
○ 20

Name: _____ Date: _____ page 1

23 twenty-three

Write the number **23**.

2 3   23

23

The number **23** can look like this.

23	23	**23**
23	*23*	Make a new **23**.

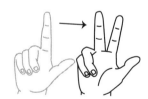

Fun With Numbers

Write the number.

 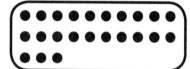

twenty-three

Circle each 23.

13   1   23   5
  23   4   9
17   21   23   6

Count up!

19 20 21 22 ____

Circle the number
that tells how many.

13   23   20

Count back!

24 ____ 22 21 20

Name: _____ Date: _____   page 3

Count Your Pennies

Color the pennies you need to buy the whistle. Write the number.

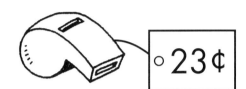

¢

_____

Count and Compare

How many crayons are in each set? Write the number. Fill in **>**, **<**, or **=**.

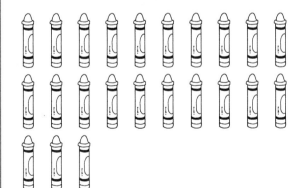

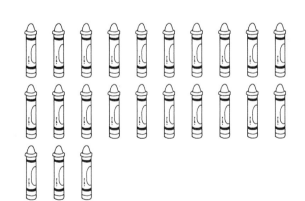

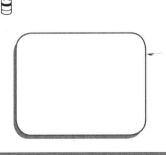

_____

What Do You Know?

What do you know about the number **23**?
Fill in the ⬜.
Use words or pictures.

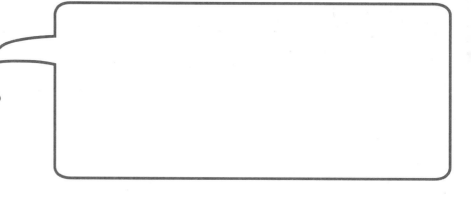

Bubble Time

Fill in the ○ to show each answer.

1. How many ▲?

   ▲ ▲ ▲ ▲ ▲ ▲ ▲ ▲ ▲ ▲
   ▲ ▲ ▲ ▲ ▲ ▲ ▲ ▲ ▲ ▲
   ▲ ▲ ▲

   ○ 20
   ○ 23
   ○ 7

2. Which numbers are missing?

   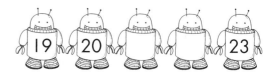

   ○ 21 and 22
   ○ 11 and 13
   ○ 6 and 7

3. Which number comes just before 23?

   ○ 6
   ○ 17
   ○ 22

4. Which number is largest?

   ○ 21
   ○ 1
   ○ 13

Name: _____ Date: _____   page 1

24 twenty-four

Write the number **24**.

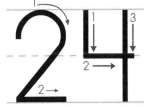

2⁴

The number **24** can look like this.

24	24	**24**
24	*24*	Make a new **24**.

Name: _____ Date: _____

Fun With Numbers

Write the number.

twenty-four

Circle each 24.

4   13   24   20
24   7   12
22   10   5   24

Count up!

21 22 23 ____ 25

Circle the number
that tells how many.

9   14   24

Count back!

26 25 ____ 23 22

Count Your Pennies

Color the pennies you need to buy the doll. Write the number.

○ 24¢

_____ ¢

Count and Compare

How many crayons are in each set? Write the number. Fill in **>**, **<**, or **=**.

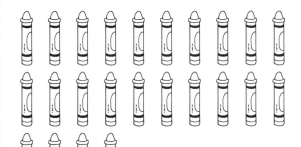

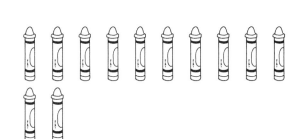

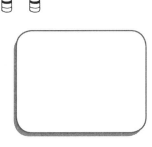

Name: _____ Date: _____ page 4

What Do You Know?

What do you know
about the number **24**?
Fill in the ☐.
Use words or pictures.

Bubble Time

Fill in the ○ to show each answer.

1. How many ▲?

▲ ▲ ▲ ▲ ▲ ▲ ▲ ▲ ▲ ▲
▲ ▲ ▲ ▲ ▲ ▲ ▲ ▲ ▲ ▲
▲ ▲ ▲ ▲

○ 24

○ 21

○ 11

2. Which numbers are missing?

○ 10 and 12

○ 21 and 23

○ 4 and 5

3. Which number comes
just before 24?

○ 9

○ 20

○ 23

4. Which number is largest?

○ 20

○ 22

○ 8

Name: _____ Date: _____ page 1

25 twenty-five

Write the number **25**.

The number **25** can look like this.

25	25	**25**
25	*25*	Make a new **25**.

Sign It!

You can use hand
shapes to make numbers.
Try making a **25**!

Fun With Numbers

Write the number.

twenty-five

Circle each 25.

24 25 10 8
12 17 25
25 19 5 21

Count up!

23 24 ____ 26 27

Circle the number
that tells how many.

15   25   5

Count back!

____ 24 23 22 21

Count Your Pennies

Color the pennies you
need to buy the paint set.
Write the number.

_____ ¢

Count and Compare

How many crayons are in each set?
Write the number. Fill in **>**, **<**, or **=**.

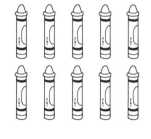

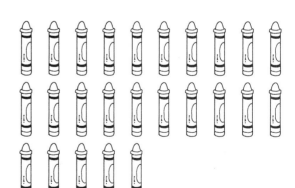

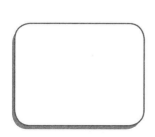

_____

Name: _____ Date: _____

What Do You Know?

What do you know about the number **25**?
Fill in the ⬜.
Use words or pictures.

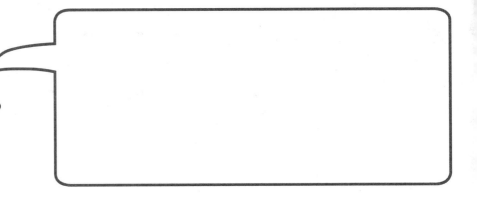

Bubble Time

Fill in the ○ to show each answer.

1. How many ▲?

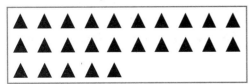

- ○ 20
- ○ 11
- ○ 25

2. Which numbers are missing?

- ○ 23 and 25
- ○ 10 and 12
- ○ 19 and 20

3. Which number comes just before 25?

- ○ 16
- ○ 24
- ○ 21

4. Which number is largest?

- ○ 23
- ○ 7
- ○ 12

Name: _____ Date: _____ page 1

 26 twenty-six

Write the number **26**.

2 6

The number **26** can look like this.

26	26	**26**
26	*26*	Make a new **26**.

Sign It!

You can use hand shapes to make numbers. Try making a **26**!

Name: _____ Date: _____ page 2

Fun With Numbers

Write the number.

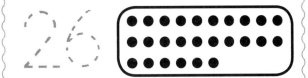

twenty-six

Circle each 26.

6   12   26   4
9   8   16
23   26   17   26

Count up!

22 23 24 25 ____

Circle the number
that tells how many.

| 26 | 16 | 20 |

Count back!

27 ____ 25 24 23

Name: _____ Date: _____ page 3

Count Your Pennies

Color the pennies you need to buy the robot. Write the number.

$\circ$ 26¢

_____ ¢

Count and Compare

How many crayons are in each set? Write the number. Fill in **>**, **<**, or **=**.

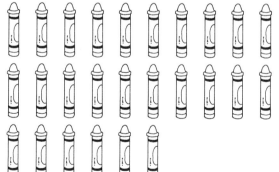

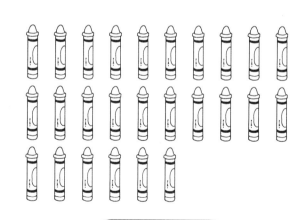

_____

Name: _____   Date: _____

What Do You Know?

What do you know about the number **26**? Fill in the ⬜. Use words or pictures.

Bubble Time   Fill in the ○ to show each answer.

1. How many ▲?

○ 15

○ 26

○ 6

2. Which numbers are missing?

○ 19 and 20

○ 12 and 13

○ 25 and 26

3. Which number comes just before 26?

○ 25

○ 21

○ 12

4. Which number is largest?

○ 18

○ 7

○ 24

Name: _____ Date: _____   page 1

27 twenty-seven

Write the number **27**.

The number **27** can look like this.

27	27	**27**
27	*27*	Make a new **27**.

Sign It!

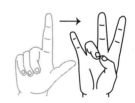

You can use hand shapes to make numbers. Try making a **27**!

Name: _____   Date: _____   page 2

Fun With Numbers

Write the number.

27 twenty-seven

Circle each 27.

17 27 20 9
10 25 27
27 15 6 7

Count up!

25 26 ____ 28 29

Circle the number
that tells how many.

7   27   21

Count back!

30 29 28 ____ 26

Name: _____ Date: _____ page 3

Count Your Pennies

Color the pennies you need to buy the top. Write the number.

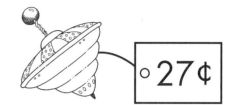

_____ ¢

Count and Compare

How many crayons are in each set? Write the number. Fill in **>**, **<**, or **=**.

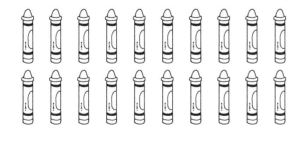

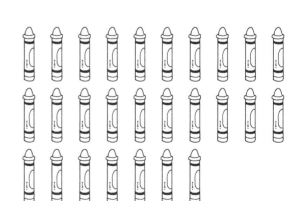

_____

Name: _____   Date: _____   page 4

What Do You Know?

What do you know about the number **27**?
Fill in the ⬛.
Use words or pictures.

Bubble Time   Fill in the ○ to show each answer.

1. How many ▲?

▲ ▲ ▲ ▲ ▲ ▲ ▲ ▲ ▲ ▲
▲ ▲ ▲ ▲ ▲ ▲ ▲ ▲ ▲
▲ ▲ ▲ ▲ ▲ ▲ ▲ ▲

○ 10
○ 20
○ 27

2. Which numbers are missing?

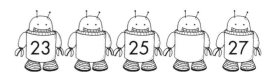

○ 12 and 14
○ 8 and 9
○ 24 and 26

3. Which number comes just before 27?

○ 20
○ 26
○ 19

4. Which number is largest?

○ 25
○ 5
○ 21

Name: _____ Date: _____

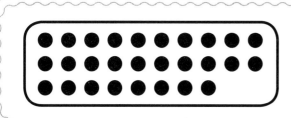

28 twenty-eight

Write the number **28**.

The number **28** can look like this.

28	28	**28**
28	*28*	Make a new **28**.

Sign It!

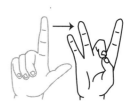

You can use hand shapes to make numbers. Try making a **28**!

Name: _____ Date: _____ page 2

Fun With Numbers

Write the number.

 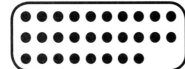

twenty-eight

Circle each 28.

1   8   14   28

28   9   22

18   28   3   27

Count up!

25 26 27 ____ 29

Circle the number
that tells how many.

8   28   12

Count back!

30 29 ____ 27 26

Name: _____ Date: _____ page 3

Count Your Pennies

Color the pennies you need to buy the ball. Write the number.

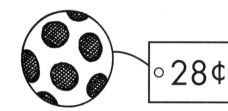

○ 28¢

_____ ¢

Count and Compare

How many crayons are in each set? Write the number. Fill in **>**, **<**, or **=**.

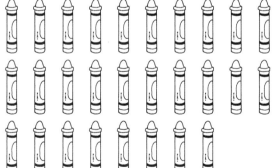

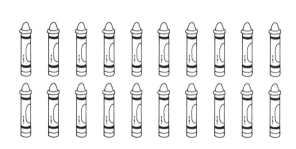

_____

Name: _____   Date: _____

What Do You Know?

What do you know about the number **28**? Fill in the ☐. Use words or pictures.

Bubble Time

Fill in the ○ to show each answer.

1. How many ▲?

   ▲ ▲ ▲ ▲ ▲ ▲ ▲ ▲ ▲ ▲
   ▲ ▲ ▲ ▲ ▲ ▲ ▲ ▲ ▲ ▲
   ▲ ▲ ▲ ▲ ▲ ▲ ▲ ▲

   ○ 15
   ○ 28
   ○ 4

2. Which numbers are missing?

   ○ 25 and 27
   ○ 14 and 15
   ○ 5 and 6

3. Which number comes just before 28?

   ○ 16
   ○ 25
   ○ 27

4. Which number is largest?

   ○ 26
   ○ 16
   ○ 3

Name: _____ Date: _____ page 1

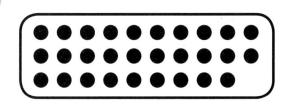

29 twenty-nine

Write the number **29**.

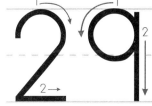

The number **29** can look like this.

29	29	**29**
29	**29**	Make a new **29**.

Sign It!

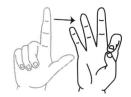

You can use hand shapes to make numbers. Try making a **29**!

Name: _____ Date: _____ page 2

Fun With Numbers

Write the number.

twenty-nine

Circle each 29.

29   3   4   18

7   29   25

20   19   15   29

Count up!

26 27 28 ____ 30

Circle the number
that tells how many.

| 29 | 2 | 19 |

Count back!

30 ____ 28 27 26

Name: _____ Date: _____

Count Your Pennies

Color the pennies you need to buy the kite. Write the number.

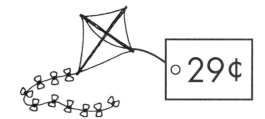

◦ 29¢

_____ ¢

Count and Compare

How many crayons are in each set? Write the number. Fill in **>**, **<**, or **=**.

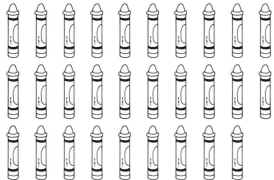

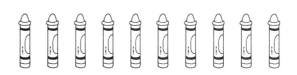

_____

21   22   23   24   25   26   27   28   29   30

29

Name: _____   Date: _____   page 4

What Do You Know?

What do you know about the number **29**?
Fill in the ☐.
Use words or pictures.

Bubble Time   Fill in the ○ to show each answer.

1. How many ▲?

▲ ▲ ▲ ▲ ▲ ▲ ▲ ▲ ▲ ▲
▲ ▲ ▲ ▲ ▲ ▲ ▲ ▲ ▲ ▲
▲ ▲ ▲ ▲ ▲ ▲ ▲ ▲ ▲

- ○ 29
- ○ 4
- ○ 11

2. Which numbers are missing?

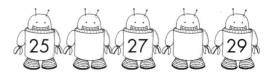

- ○ 6 and 8
- ○ 26 and 28
- ○ 21 and 23

3. Which number comes just before 29?

- ○ 13
- ○ 28
- ○ 24

4. Which number is largest?

- ○ 9
- ○ 12
- ○ 27

Name: _____ Date: _____

30   thirty

Write the number **30**.

3 0

The number **30** can look like this.

30	30	**30**
30	***30***	Make a new **30**.

Sign It!

You can use hand shapes to make numbers. Try making a **30**!

Fun With Numbers

Write the number.

30

thirty

Circle each 30.

2   27   3   30
30   20   10
13   1   30   29

Count up!

26 27 28 29 _____

Circle the number that tells how many.

10   20   30

Count back!

_____ 29 28 27 26

Instant Practice Packets: Numbers & Counting • © 2011 by Joan Novelli & Holly Grundon • Scholastic Teaching Resources

Count Your Pennies

Color the pennies you need to buy the glove. Write the number.

∘ 30¢

_____ ¢

Count and Compare

How many crayons are in each set? Write the number. Fill in **>**, **<**, or **=**.

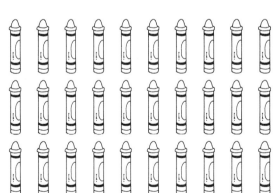

_____

Name: _____   Date: _____

What Do You Know?

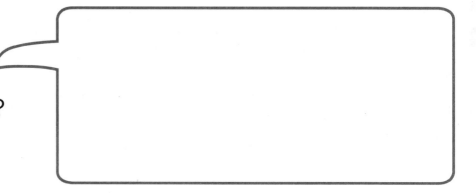

What do you know about the number **30**?
Fill in the ☐.
Use words or pictures.

Bubble Time

Fill in the ○ to show each answer.

1. How many ▲?

   ▲ ▲ ▲ ▲ ▲ ▲ ▲ ▲ ▲ ▲
   ▲ ▲ ▲ ▲ ▲ ▲ ▲ ▲ ▲ ▲
   ▲ ▲ ▲ ▲ ▲ ▲ ▲ ▲ ▲ ▲

   ○ 20
   ○ 10
   ○ 30

2. Which numbers are missing?

   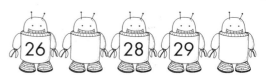

   ○ 27 and 30
   ○ 15 and 18
   ○ 8 and 9

3. Which number comes just before 30?

   ○ 25
   ○ 29
   ○ 11

4. Which number is largest?

   ○ 6
   ○ 28
   ○ 14